WHO? WHAT? WHY?

It's a funny old world!

Ever had a strange feeling? I'm Sparky the dog and I'd like to welcome you to *Who? What? Why?* In this edition of *The Navigator*, I'll introduce you to some fascinating people. Many of them are famous for doing some weird and wonderful things, which may seem a little bit bonkers to us. You'll hear about some people who take making funny faces quite seriously, and you'll get to meet the amazing Harry Houdini, a rather slippery escape artist. I'll also take you on a trip to Easter Island, where you'll see some very strange stone statues.

Prepare to be amazed!

Text Type	Literacy Skills	Wider Curriculum Links
Report	Deductive comprehension; questioning; responding to the text	**Geography** Unit 10: A village in India
Letter: Recount	Deductive comprehension; making comparisons; interrogating text	**History** Unit 6A: Why have people invaded and settled in Britain in the past?
Letter: Explanation	Understanding point of view; facts given in a fictional format; questioning; understanding audience	**Science** Unit 4B: Habitats
Report	Comparing data; understanding audience and purpose of writing; comparing different ways of giving information	**Geography** Unit 8: Improving the environment
Recount	Distinguishing between fact and opinion; spoken and written language; making links with own experiences	**History** Unit 9: What was it like for children in the Second World War?
Explanation/ Recount	Finding interesting facts; close reading; thinking about reasons	**History** Unit 6A: Why have people invaded and settled in Britain in the past?
Explanation	Scanning; finding interesting facts	
Recount	Justifying opinions; understanding and expressing point of view	**PSHE:** Preparing to play an active role as citizens
Recount	Scanning; finding interesting facts	
Report	Summarising information; distinguishing between fact and opinion	
Fun spread		
		ICT: Year 4 Schemes of work

What happens to the money you collect for Comic Relief on Red Nose Day? Some of it goes towards making a chocolate bar called Dubble! Dubble is special because the cocoa it contains is grown and sold under a system called Fair Trade.

COMIC RELIEF

A village in Ghana

The Cocoa Farmers

The farmers who grow the cocoa for Dubble live in Ghana, on the west coast of Africa. Most of Ghana's cocoa farmers earn no more than £100 a year, so in 1993 some farmers grouped together to form Kuapa Kokoo, a co-operative that helps them get a better price for their cocoa. Comic Relief gave Kuapa Kokoo money to help them organise the co-operative.

A Fair Price

Kuapa Kokoo now has 35000 members. They sell cocoa to the Day Chocolate Company in the UK, which is the company that makes Dubble. The Day Company pay Kuapa Kokoo a fair price for the cocoa so more money goes back to the farmers, their families and their villages.

Lynda showing us the cocoa pods that are used to make Dubble bars

Twelve-year-old Lynda Agyman lives in Ghana. This is what she told Comic Relief:

"My dad is a cocoa farmer, and I know quite a bit about cocoa farming because I already help out in the cocoa fields. I started helping my dad when I was eight. It gets very busy, especially at harvest time, when the cocoa pods are ripe and you have to slice them off the tree trunks.

Collecting water from a well

"I go to school nearby. I collect water on the way home, and help with cooking. I have to work fast so that I finish in time to do my homework. Once the sun has gone down, I work by the light of a hurricane lamp, because we don't have electricity.

"My dad is a member of the Kuapa Kokoo co-operative, which means that we're treated fairly. Kuapa Kokoo is really good cocoa — it's the best! We say our cocoa is 'Pa Pa Paa!', which means 'best of the best'. When I'm helping on the farm I'll think of you eating it, and when you eat it, think of me too!"

You can help Kuapa Kokoo by giving to Comic Relief and by buying Dubble bars — that's double help! You will find Dubble in most supermarkets.

Marcus Aulus
to his mother, greetings

We have now arrived in the
north of England, at Housesteads
Fort on the Great Wall, built by
our legions at the order of the
Emperor Hadrian. By the gods,
it is cold here, and very wet!
Please can you send me some
thick socks and a thicker tunic.

Home sweet home!

I wish I knew why we were here.
The weather is bad. The people
this side of the Wall are bad-tempered
barbarians. On the other side of the Wall,
the barbarians are even worse — war-like and savage.

Our centurion says we came because we heard that
Britain was rich and full of things we wanted like tin,
precious metals and pearls. And, as we all know, the
Emperor Claudius badly needed to conquer somewhere
in order to look like a good emperor. Well, Claudius did
conquer Britain, and then Hadrian built his Wall, to keep
the northern barbarians out.

I cannot see much sign of Britain being full of anything at all, except for mud. The barbarians even cover the outside of their low, dark, smoky huts with mud – to stop the wind whistling in. The fort, I am glad to say, is well-run and has a bathhouse and a proper toilet. This is a good thing, for the barbarians do not understand the need to be clean at all. They do not seem to wash their hair or bodies from one year's end to the next, nor do they shave!

I am sorry to complain, Mother, for a good soldier does not complain. I am sure we will get used to this place. It may even stop raining ... When you send the socks and tunic, could you also send some wine? The barbarians do not drink it. They drink some awful sweet stuff called mead. It makes you very sick. Perhaps some money, too, as there is not much else to do with our free time but play at dice.

Cold wet Britain!

Farewell, your son,

Marcus

Dear Giant Panda ...

Dear Giant Panda

Last week, I saw a picture of you in the newspaper. I thought I would write and tell you that soon my class and I are doing a walk for wildlife. We are raising funds to help endangered species, and I wondered how you are doing. Did you know that you are a symbol for wildlife conservation? But my teacher says giant pandas are still at risk. Is that true?

Love from Lucy

Me and my favourite snack

Dear Lucy

Yes, we are officially an endangered species because there are fewer than a thousand of us living in the wild now. We live in China, in bamboo forests on steep mountains, a few thousand metres high. We used to live lower down the mountains, but people have settled there now, so we have lost some of our habitat.

Love from Giant Panda

Since 1987, giant pandas have lost almost a third of their natural habitat.

Dear Giant Panda

My teacher says you are endangered because you only eat bamboo. Is that right? I like so many different foods!

Love from Lucy ✗

Dear Lucy

Your teacher is almost right! We do eat meat now and again, but mostly we eat bamboo - about twelve to eighteen kilograms every day! Every so often bamboos flower and then die. It can take up to twenty years before there is a new crop that we can feed on. In the past, when one crop died, we just moved on to find more on another mountain top. But now people live in the valleys below us, so we cannot move around so easily. If the bamboo dies where we live, we can starve.

There are poachers who hunt us illegally, too.

Good luck with your walk!

Love from Giant Panda

Dear Giant Panda

Thank you for your letters. Think of us next week. We will be taking giant steps for giant pandas!

Love from Lucy ✗

There are around 6500 species of endangered animals. Their natural habitats are being destroyed for logging or farming. Many are also being illegally hunted, or poached.

Revolting Rubbish!

8% RECYCLED

9% INCINERATED

83% LANDFILL

- Just 8% of our waste is recycled.
- 9% is burned in incinerators.
- 83% is dumped in big holes in the ground called landfill sites.

The waste we produce every day in the UK would fill London's Trafalgar Square right up to the top of Nelson's Column. It adds up to around 28 million tonne a year – that's 500 kilograms of rubbish for every one of us.

21% of household waste is organic waste, such as vegetables and other food. Rotting food attracts scavengers such as rats, foxes and seagulls. It can degrade to form a stinking, polluting liquid.

In the UK, we throw away around 12 million cans each year. If they were placed end to end, they would reach to the moon and back.

Thousands of dirty nappies containing tonnes of raw sewage are thrown away in plastic bags every day. The average child wears 6500 nappies before they are potty-trained.

Rotting rubbish produces stinking gases that are increasing global warming. It produces 55% methane and 45% carbon dioxide. Methane can build up and cause explosions.

Over six million kilometres of aluminium foil are thrown away each year. That would be enough to wrap around the planet 164 times.

Chemicals, heavy metals and bacteria can leak into the soil from landfill sites, and contaminate our water.

Each year, the average UK family uses around six trees' worth of paper.

Glass and plastics do not rot down or decay. Broken glass is dangerous for people and wildlife. Plastic bags have been found around the necks of strangled birds and in cows' stomachs.

So what can we do to reduce the amount of waste we produce?
- Recycle paper, glass, plastics, cans and clothes
- Buy recycled goods
- Turn vegetable and garden waste into compost
- Avoid wasteful packaging and disposable products

An Evacuee Remembers...

Sam:

Miss Green says we're starting a project about evacuees in school tomorrow, Grandma. What's an evacuee?

Grandma:

I was an evacuee, sweetheart, during the war, the Second World War, that started in 1939. I was just eight. All us kids were sent away from London, in case there was bombing. That's what an evacuee was – a kid who was sent away from their home to somewhere safe.

Sam:

So did you go with your Mum and Dad?

Grandma:

No, with our school. I went from London to Wareham, in Dorset.

Sam:

Did you all stay together?

Grandma:

No. We went on the train together, then to a big hall where people came and picked who they wanted. We got split up.

Some kids weren't picked because they were with their brothers and sisters, and their mums had said they had to stick together.

London child bombed out

12

Lots of the people who had said they'd have an evacuee only wanted to take one kid.

Sam:

What happened to you?

Grandma:

I was lucky, 'cos I was on my own. The vicar's wife from Holmbridge village chose me 'cos she said I looked the cleanest.

Sam:

That was **very** rude of her!

Grandma:

Yes, sweetheart, it was, but we were very poor and where we lived it was hard to keep clean. There wasn't proper running water and families lived all crammed together. Lots of the kids had fleas and nits. My brothers and sisters were grown up, so it was just me and Mum and Dad. Mum was very particular about being clean. I probably had nits, cos of sitting with the others and all that.

Sam:

Did you like being an evacuee?

Grandma:

Well, yes and no. The food was good and I had a nice room and the vicar and his wife were kind, but they had lots of rules you had to keep. It was very strange living in the country. I'd never seen a cow – I'd no idea they were so big! I missed Mum and Dad. I wrote home and Mum visited a few times. I was glad to go back home at the end of the war.

One of the first things the Romans did after they invaded Britain was to build roads to connect the main towns. Roman roads were hard work to build. The ground had to be flattened and dug out. A layer of gravel was put down, then paving was carefully laid on top so that rainwater ran off to the sides. The roads ran straight, so bridges had to be built over rivers.

So why did the Romans go to all this trouble? Anthony, a road surveyor in the Roman army, is here to explain.

ROMAN ROADS

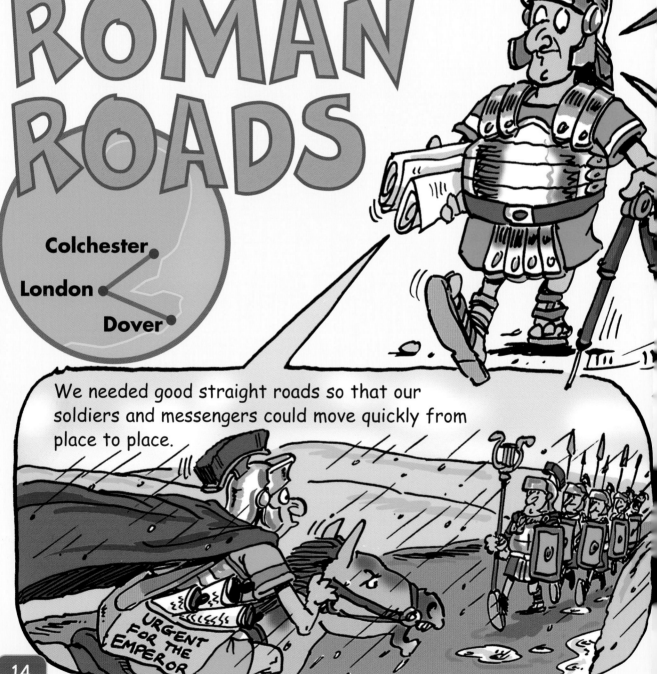

Colchester

London

Dover

We needed good straight roads so that our soldiers and messengers could move quickly from place to place.

URGENT FOR THE EMPEROR

Before we built our roads, it was hard to move supplies around, especially in winter. The heavy carts got bogged down in the mud.

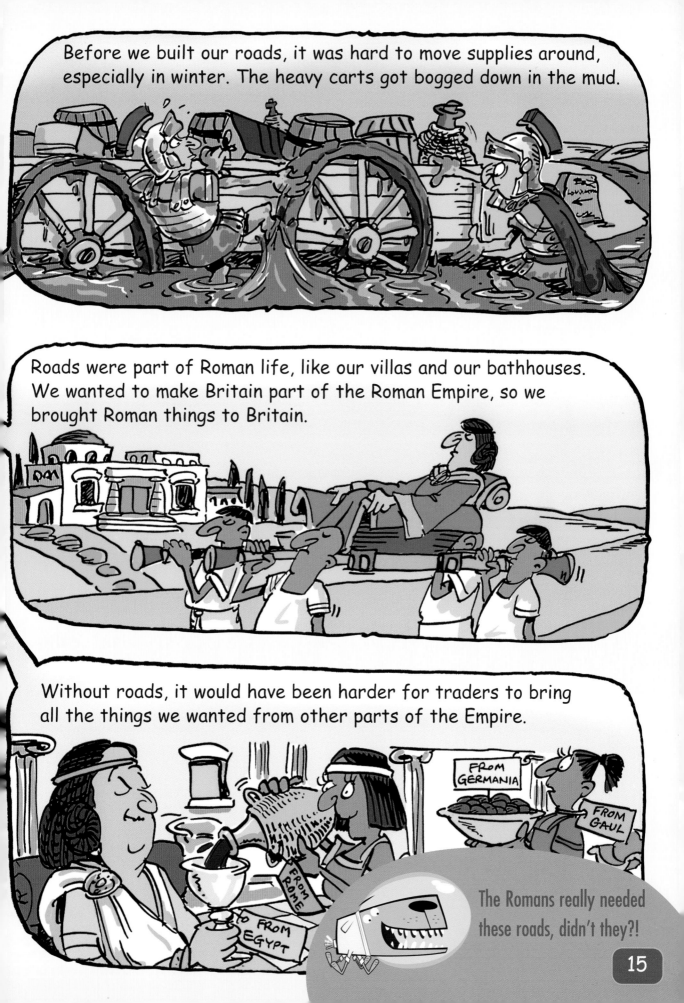

Roads were part of Roman life, like our villas and our bathhouses. We wanted to make Britain part of the Roman Empire, so we brought Roman things to Britain.

Without roads, it would have been harder for traders to bring all the things we wanted from other parts of the Empire.

FROM GERMANIA

FROM GAUL

FROM ROME

FROM EGYPT

The Romans really needed these roads, didn't they?!

MYSTERY IN STONE

About 4000 kilometres off the coast of South America, in the middle of the Pacific Ocean, lies a small island with a big secret. On this island, called Easter Island, are hundreds of giant figures carved out of stone. Archaeologists believe that some of the figures were carved nearly 2000 years ago. But why, and how, did the islanders build these statues?

STRANGE STATUES

The people who live on Easter Island call the statues *moai*, which means 'image'. The moai are all very similar. They all have long heads on thick bodies, and hold their arms tight against their bodies. Their eyes are set deep into their faces, their chins jut out and they have long ears. Some of the moai have crowns on their heads. The smallest statues are about three metres high, but others are as tall as ten metres. The largest moai weighs as much as twelve elephants!

THE MOAI TODAY

HOW WERE THE MOAI BUILT?

The stones for the moai came from a volcano called Rano Raraku, which is in the middle of Easter Island. Archaeologists believe that the islanders moved the huge stones from the volcano to the shore using logs. They rolled the stones over the logs, which made them easier to move. The islanders then stood the stones up along the shore, and used pointed stone picks to carve them into moai.

WHY ALL THE HARD WORK?

The people of Easter Island believe that the moai represent their chiefs. They are all built with their backs to the sea, guarding the villages on the island.

Archaeologists believe that there were originally as many as 600 moai. Over the years, many of them have become damaged. Since the 1950s, archaeologists have been working with the islanders to restore the moai, so that future generations can marvel at these amazing statues.

·S·T·O·R·Y· ·C·H·A·R·A·C·T·E·R· ·C·R·I·M·E·S·

Characters from three famous stories stand accused of crimes: a wicked fairy, a wolf, and two tailors. Are they guilty of these crimes? If so, how should they be punished?

·S·L·E·E·P·I·N·G· ·B·E·A·U·T·Y·

The Queen of a distant country gave birth to a baby girl. At the feast to celebrate, the country's six good fairies wished the baby great beauty, a long life, and love. But the King had forgotten to invite the seventh fairy, who was lonely and miserable. The fairy, miffed at not being invited, cast an evil spell on the baby. She would one day prick herself on a needle and die. Fortunately, one of the good fairies weakened the spell, so that the young princess would not die, but would sleep for a hundred years.

The Accused:
The uninvited fairy

The Crime: Laying bad wishes on defenceless kids

Mitigating Circumstances:
Advanced age and/or senility

A hungry wolf wanted to kill a sheep for his dinner, but all the sheep in the field ran away whenever he drew near. He found an old sheepskin and pulled it over himself as a disguise. He approached the sheep, and they didn't run away. The shepherd drove his sheep (including the disguised wolf) into the pen and went home for the night. Now the sheep were at the wolf's mercy. He could pounce on any he liked, and feast to his heart's content.

The Accused: The wolf

The Crime: Stealing sheep with intent to kill

Mitigating Circumstances: Nature of the beast

·T·H·E··E·M·P·E·R·O·R·'S··N·E·W··C·L·O·T·H·E·S·

Two tailors went to the Emperor saying they had a special cloth which only clever people could see and feel. The Emperor paid them to make a suit for him. The Emperor could not see or feel the clothes, but as he did not want to seem stupid, he pretended he could. Also wanting to seem clever, everyone at the parade said how magnificent the Emperor looked. Then one boy in the crowd cried out, "The Emperor's absolutely starkers!" Everyone realised that there was no suit at all, and the Emperor ordered the imprisonment of the two tailors.

The Accused: The two tailors **The Crime:** Fraud

Mitigating Circumstances:
The stupid Emperor deserved everything he got

EVERYDAY INVENTIONS

IN YOUR BEST HANDWRITING, PLEASE!

Ballpoint pen

Teachers in the past must have had a terrible time getting children to write neatly! From around the seventh century onwards, people wrote with quills. Quills broke easily, and they were really messy!

In 1884 an American named L E Waterman finally invented a fountain pen that didn't leak. However, in 1938 a breakthrough was made. A Hungarian journalist called Laszlo Biro noticed that the ink used for newspapers did not smudge, but he couldn't get it to flow through a fountain pen. So he created the ballpoint pen which allowed the printing ink to flow round a steel ball.

Zip Up

The first zips weren't used for doing up your trousers, but keeping shoes on your feet. The first attempt – the 'Clasp Locker' of 1893 – failed. The second version – the 'Separable Fastener' – was heavier and had more teeth. It became known as a 'zipper' because of the sound it made, and was used as a fastener on rubber boots!

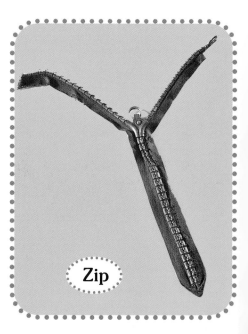
Zip

CALL THIS A BIKE?

The first 'bicycle' didn't have any pedals – you just pushed your way along, leaning from side to side to steer! In fact, it took about another fifty years for a bicycle that we would recognise today to be developed.

1790
The first bicycle is invented in France.

1816
German inventor von Draise creates the draisine, steered by the handlebars.

1839
Scottish blacksmith K Macmillan adds pedals.

1855
The boneshaker becomes famous for causing accidents.

1900s
Smaller rubber tyres, gears and brakes make for a safer ride.

1981
The first commercially successful mountain bike becomes available.

Some of the things people do seem quite mad to the rest of us. For instance...

Swimming in grease

A man and woman cover themselves with thick grease to swim the English Channel. Wacky or what? Let's see. The record for swimming the Channel is around seven hours, but most swimmers take much longer. Quite a while to spend in very cold water! This is where the grease comes in. It helps keep the cold out. So perhaps it's not so mad after all. Why anyone would want to swim the English Channel is something else again...

WACKY THINGS

High flyers

A man lies in a wooden cradle and tries to fly. What on earth is he doing that for? This happened a very long time ago, in December 1903, and the man is an American called Orville Wright. Orville and his brother Wilbur were the first to build and fly a powered aircraft. If they hadn't done this we might not have the huge, powerful planes of today, which can fly all around the world!

Bedtime blues

A woman deliberately tries to keep awake night after night. Why? She's taking part in a carefully monitored sleep deprivation experiment. Scientists want to know how long a human being can go without sleep. They have discovered that without enough sleep we lose body temperature and the ability to think or function properly. It also makes us yearn for our beds.

Every day, all over the world, people dress up as chickens, Count Dracula, Martians, and anything else you can think of. Can so many people be out of their minds? Not at all! They are going to fancy dress parties. People have been dressing up in weird outfits for hundreds of years. In the sixteenth century, for instance, men wore tights and hats with feathers in them. But that wasn't fancy dress. That was considered normal then!

Fancy that!

PEOPLE DO...

Strange faces

Everyone pulls faces from time to time, but some people take face-pulling quite seriously. They call it 'gurning'. In the World Gurning Championships, contestants pull faces while wearing a horse collar. The ugliest expression wins. The story goes that in olden days a horse collar (or braffin) was put on the village idiot, who would then pull grotesque faces in return for a pint of beer. Seems a fair exchange...

EGREMONT CRAB FAIR

Can you think of any wacky things that people do in order to break world records?
See if you can find out any information about some unusual record breakers.

Incredible but true!

Prepare to be amazed when you read the following newspaper and magazine articles about some astonishing feats. Wow!

Heart Attack Man Saves Boy!

A quiet stroll in the park turned into quite an adventure for 56-year-old Arnold Learner. After hearing a cry for help coming from the children's playground, Learner rushed to the area to investigate. There, he was met with the sight of a young boy trapped under a heavy iron pipe. Learner quickly lifted the pipe and saved the boy's life. The hero's actions were especially amazing considering the heart attack he had suffered six years earlier. Learner said, "I didn't really think about how heavy the pipe was when I picked it up, but afterwards I guessed it must weigh about 150 kilograms."

After the incident, Learner's sons, a reporter and a police officer all tried unsuccessfully to lift the pipe, which actually weighed over 800 kilograms.

Arnold Learner

How did he do it?

Our scientist says:

"In times of stress, your body can perform amazing feats of strength. When your mind senses danger, your body has an automatic alarm that lets you use the full power of your resources."

HOUDINI

Escapes Death Again!

Harry Houdini has yet again been amazing Americans with his daring feats. The people of Detroit were treated to a spectacle when Houdini climbed to the top of the bridge over the Detroit River. After looking down at a small hole in the ice, the great escape artist raised his handcuffed wrists and then proceeded to dive into the icy water.

After several minutes many people began to look worried as there had still been no sign of the escape artist. "The shock of the icy water would kill someone," commented a concerned Detroit doctor.

After eight minutes, a diver prepared to enter the water to look for Houdini. As he was climbing down a rope into the water, Houdini's hands and head bobbed above the surface. The people of Detroit greeted the amazing escape artist with cheers.

How did he do it?

Our reporter spoke to Houdini after his miraculous escape. **"After I got the handcuffs off,**

Houdini had escaped again!

I lost the opening in the ice. I had to float near the surface and use the air between the ice and the water to breathe. I gulped some air and then went back under to look for the light from the opening." Houdini's ability to control his body helps him perform amazing feats. He always eats the right food and he exercises frequently. He takes ice baths to get his body used to freezing conditions, and practises breathing very slowly.

Byte-Sized ICT

Dear Giant Panda ...

Symbol designs

If you saw a symbol like this, what would you think of? The panda is used as a symbol for wildlife conservation, worldwide. A symbol or logo has to be clear, simple and easy to recognise, so that people remember what it stands for whenever they see it.

Be a graphic designer and use an art or graphics package on your computer to design a new symbol for an environmental issue. You could come up with one for recycling or stopping pollution, or why not think of a new one for wildlife conservation, using another endangered animal. Some other endangered animals include tigers and whales.

Remember to keep it clear and simple, using only two or three colours. Bold colours and shapes are best. Avoid too many details.

A Roman soldier writes home

Roman reply

Can you put yourself in someone else's shoes? Why not try to imagine you are the mother of the Roman soldier, Marcus, from pages 6 and 7?

Use a word-processor to type a reply to your son, to keep his spirits up. You could tell him what has been going on back home. Remember to tell him what you are sending with the letter. Set out your letter clearly, using a new paragraph for each topic you write to him about.

Helpful hint!

If you have forgotten to use paragraphs, you can put them in afterwards. First, move the cursor to the beginning of the sentence where a new paragraph should start (using the mouse or the arrow keys). Then press 'return' twice. Remember to move the cursor back to the end of the writing when you have finished, if you want to type some more.

Comic relief

Comic relief research challenge

Where else does the money for Comic Relief go? Can you find out using the Internet? If you manage to find some useful information about where it goes, print it out and then use a highlighter pen to pick out the key facts.

Helpful hint!

The web addresses of charities usually end in .org.uk

Wacky things people do ...

Record research

Can you find out three more weird, wonderful or dangerous things people have done to try and break a record? Use the Internet to search for some more interesting record-breakers!

Print out your information, read what the person did to a friend, and ask them to guess what the record was set at.

Everyday inventions

Pen timeline game

How much do your friends know about the history of the pen? Now's your chance to find out. Use the information on page 20 to help you type a short description of what pens were like and how they were used. You could include something about pens today, such as the invention of smelly gel pens!

Leave plenty of space between each fact and don't include any dates. You could add some clip-art, (for example, of a quill), for the earliest kind of pen. Print out your facts, cut them up, and then ask a friend to put them in order from the earliest kind of pen to the most modern.

When you have finished, you could make them into a time line for pen development up to today.

Story character crimes

Wanted!

Some of those fairy tale characters are just so wicked! They are the most wanted characters in fairy land! Choose a 'baddie' from a fairy tale (you'll find some ideas on pages 18 and 19) and design a 'wanted' poster, using a publishing software or a word-processing package on your computer.

You will need to make it clear enough to be read from a distance. Try a few test prints and check your font size is big enough. Include a few details about the baddie's appearance and why he or she is 'wanted'.

Ever fancied being the villain in a fairy tale? Here's your chance. Try dressing up as the character you chose and get a friend to take a digital picture to insert into your poster. If you don't have a digital camera, add a picture using clip-art or scan one in from a story book.

Glossary

archaeologist	someone who studies ancient remains, usually by excavation
bacteria	tiny living things which sometimes cause disease
carbon dioxide	the gas formed when the carbon in food and fuel is burned and combined with oxygen
centurian	the commander of a company of men in ancient Rome. The company was originally a 'century' (100 men)
conservation	taking good care of things around us, especially things that can easily disappear and cannot be replaced
contaminate	to pollute or infect
co-operative	a community that produces and distributes goods, sharing the profits
endangered species	animals and plants that are so rare they will become extinct if they are not protected
evacuee	someone who has to be moved from a dangerous place to a safe place
Fair Trade	a system of trading that makes sure people in developing countries are paid a fair price for what they make or grow

habitat	the place where a particular animal or plant, or community of animals and plants, lives
incinerate	to burn refuse to ashes
landfill	a large area of waste land that is set aside to bury rubbish
legion	a unit of the Roman army, including soldiers on horseback
mead	alcoholic drink made of fermented honey and water
mitigating (circumstances)	circumstances that may explain why someone did something wrong
poacher	someone who captures animals by illegal means
quill	the hollow stem of a feather, once used as a pen
recycle	to turn household waste into material that can be re-used
tunic	ancient Roman short-sleeved body garment reaching to the knees

Index